BRANCH LINE TO HEMEL HEMPSTEAD

Sue and Geoff Woodward

MP Middleton Press

Cover photographs:

Front: Class 4 2-6-0 no. 43119 steams gently as it stands in the passing loop at Heath Park Depot, on l0th March 1956. The track here was laid on the short stretch of embankment beside Cotterells Road, which was the first stretch of the original line to be built. (B.Connell)

Back: Viewed from Adeyfield Road bridge, class 4 no. 43118 drifts gently into Hemel Hempstead station in May 1962, with its train of empty vans. (S.Summerson)

Published October 2006

ISBN 1 904474 88 8

© Middleton Press, 2006

Design Deborah Esher

Published by
> *Middleton Press*
> *Easebourne Lane*
> *Midhurst, West Sussex*
> *GU29 9AZ*

Tel: 01730 813169
Fax: 01730 812601
Email: info@middletonpress.co.uk
www.middletonpress.co.uk

Printed & bound by Biddles Ltd, Kings Lynn

INDEX

61	Beaumont's Halt	19	Harpenden Junction
116	Boxmoor	99	Heath Park Halt
70	Claydale Sidings	83	Hemel Hempstead
75	Godwin's Halt	49	Redbourn
1	Harpenden	39	Roundwood Halt

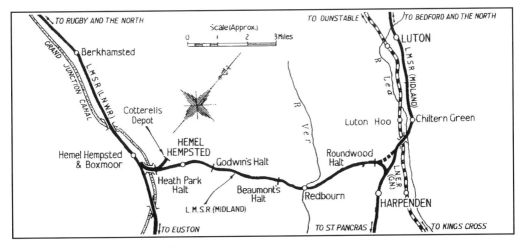

Related lines in 1945.
(Railway Magazine)

ACKNOWLEDGEMENTS

We are grateful to all those who have allowed us to use their photographs in this publication and are particularly appreciative of the extra help given by many of those named.

GEOGRAPHICAL SETTING

The route is entirely on the dip slope of the Chiltern Hills, which are composed of Chalk. The branch starts west of the valley of the River Lea, which runs east to eventually flow into the Thames in East London.

A climb over a ridge brings the route into the upper part of the valley of the small River Ver at Redbourn. A further area of high ground is traversed before the final descent into Hemel Hempstead and the end of passenger operation at Heath Park. The town is situated at the confluence of the River Bulbourne and the River Gade.

I. The entire branch is shown on the 1945 edition at 1ins to 1 mile.

HISTORICAL BACKGROUND

The origins of this line date back to the early 1860s. At that time the Great Northern Railway, following the Lea Valley, provided a station on Harpenden's eastern outskirts but the Midland Railway's new main line from Bedford to London, although under construction, was still several years from opening. Therefore, it is to Hemel Hempstead we must turn for the inspiration behind this cross-country railway. Because local landowners, the Boxmoor Trust, had forced both the Grand Junction (later Grand Union) Canal and the London & Birmingham Railway (later the London & North Western) to build well away from the small market town of Hemel Hempstead, it found itself isolated from the benefits of either means of transport. There were, however, developing businesses in the town and surrounding areas which could make use of such facilities. Local supporters formed the Hemel Hempsted & London & North Western Railway Company and an Act of Parliament, passed on 13th July 1863, allowed for a 1¾ mile long railway from Hemel Hempstead town to the LNWR station at Boxmoor. From this time forward, all railway references to Hemel Hempstead left out the "a" until the 1960s.

However, another Act, passed on the 16th July 1866, enabled the line to be extended to join the Midland Railway at Harpenden junction, with a station at Redbourn en route. Eventually, the first passenger train ran on 16th July 1877, from Hemel Hempstead to Harpenden and north to Luton.

The line's advantages were said to be cheaper coal and the convenience of taking the local cottage-industry straw plait to the plait halls in Luton.

The only way forward for the HH&LNWR was to hand the line over to the MR, on a fixed rental, dropping any thoughts of associating with the LNWR, or the GNR at Harpenden. It was thus left with no branch station at Harpenden and the stretch of newly-constructed line between Hemel Hempstead and Boxmoor stations lay idle. However, when a new gas works was constructed at Boxmoor in 1880, the MR undertook to supply coal and a siding was built to connect with the previously unused section. In the Cotterells area, a remnant of the short line was also connected to provide sidings.

The MR totally absorbed the route in 1886 and almost immediately received representations from local businessmen, who were seeking to travel to London without first going into Luton. The company accordingly agreed to alter the junction with the main line to give a south-facing curve so that branch trains could run into Harpenden station. This opened on 2nd July 1888.

Further alterations were made in 1905 when Beaumont's Halt, Godwin's Halt and Heath Park Halt were built, to coincide with the start of a rail-motor service. This was the first time passenger trains had ventured west of Hemel Hempstead station and created the unusual situation of a halt being the passenger terminus.

The MR was absorbed into the London, Midland & Scottish Railway in 1923, who authorised the construction of Roundwood Halt (in a developing area of Harpenden), opening on 8th August 1927. Not long after, the LMS found it necessary to reduce expenditure and considered implementing a service run by a Ro-Railer, a vehicle with wheels and tyres, as well as traditional rail wheels. During 1930 such a vehicle was tested on the roads between Watford and Hemel Hempstead and from there by rail to Redbourn.

However, back in 1923 the LMS had also taken over the LNWR bus service, which it continued to run between Boxmoor and Hemel Hempstead stations. On 18th February 1929, a Leyland bus extended this service, with eleven intermediate stops, to Harpenden station. Within a month the rail service had been reduced to two trains daily in each direction. Following WWII, the LMS made even more severe cutbacks and 'temporarily suspended' the branch passenger service on 16th June 1947. It was never reinstated.

Whilst the line had always failed to attract large numbers of passengers (apart from the many specials which were organised from Hemel Hempstead), it was of great use to local manufacturers, farmers and watercress growers. Of course, coal was transported in large quantities for the gasworks and local merchants, and this continued after British Railways took over, following nationalisation in 1948.

Following a government decision to create a new town at Hemel Hempstead, the section between the station and the gasworks was closed and taken over by the Hemel Hempstead New Town Development Corporation on 31st August 1959. So that the gasworks could go on receiving coal, a connection was laid into Boxmoor goods yard, opening when the other section was severed

- at last securing the link which the HH&LNWR had in its sights so many years before. It had a short life, though, as the gasworks closed on 1st April 1960.

The redundant track was lifted from Heath Park Goods Depot early that year, followed by the section up to Hemel Hempstead station. On 1st July 1963 the goods station closed, as did Godwins Sidings on 2nd March 1964. Buildings were demolished and the track lifted as far as Claydale Sidings, where a buffer stop was installed, leaving the remainder of the track through to Harpenden, although showing signs of age and neglect.

The Hemel Hempstead Lightweight Concrete Co., Ltd., (shortened to Hemelite) took over the old brickworks attached to Claydale Sidings in 1958 to manufacture building blocks. New equipment was installed and the sidings were completely relaid, using secondhand track, in 1959. The basic ingredient of the blocks was ash from power stations in the Midlands, which was delivered by British Rail until 1968. At that time BR wished to cease all workings on the former branch line, but reached agreement with Hemelite that they could operate it, reduced to siding status, and this they did from lst February 1968.

On Saturday 16th July 1977 the centenary of the branch was marked by events at both ends

of the line and one of Hemelite's shunting engines transported a group of enthusiasts to Harpenden, to attend a celebratory exhibition in the Library. Other 'specials' were organised unofficially during their time as lessees of the line.

BR's intention to electrify the main line tolled the death-knell for the branch line and Hemelite accepted its last delivery of ash by rail on 28th June 1979, shunting the empty wagons back the next day. The "Nickey Line" was no more ....

Why the Nickey Line? This is a nickname which has been applied to this line from the time it was under construction - and yet no-one has been able to discover from whence it came. Many theories have been put forward, such as the line being in the Parish of St. Nicholas, the navvies that built it wore knickerbockers or the exhaust of the engines sounded like a much-repeated "knickerbocker, knickerbocker" as they climbed the steep gradient up to Roundwood. Some of these, and many of the others can be discounted because they could only apply once the line was open, but it is a fact the name only applied to the Harpenden end of the line. In Hemel Hempstead people referred to "Puffing Annie" or "Gentle Annie". What we do know is that the earliest printed references to the Nickey Line included the 'e' - so shall we.

PASSENGER SERVICES

The initial service comprised four trains, weekdays only, between Luton and Hemel Hempstead, but this frequency was soon reduced to three. We have no records of trains running on Sundays.

It was increased to seven in July 1888, following the establishment of Harpenden as the starting point for branch trains. However, one journey commenced at St Pancras at 9.0am for many years and was provided by a slipcoach from

an express.

From August 1895, nine trips were operated on the branch, this being reduced to eight in about 1908 and to seven by 1922.

Drastic cuts came on 4th March 1929, after which time there were only two return journeys, although there were two extra on Saturdays until World War II. This minimal service remained until withdrawn on 16th June 1947.

May 1889

HARPENDEN and HEMEL HEMPSTED.—Midland.

Miles	Down. St. Pancras Sta.,	Week Days.											NOTES.
		mrn	mrn	aft	aft	aft	aft	aft					
576	London ....dep.	6 53	9 2	1 1	5 2	1 4	0 5	10	6 33	8 40			¶ "Halts" at Beaumont's and Godwin's, between Redbourn and Hemel Hempsted; and Heath Park, beyond Hemel Hempsted.
—	Harpenden ....dep.	7 58	10 28	1 46	3 12	4 42	5 56	7 20	9 27				
3¼	Redbourn ¶	8 8	10 31	1 57	3 23	4 53	6 7	7 31	9 38				
8	Hemel Hempsted ¶ arr.	8 23	10 46	2 12	3 37	5 7	6 21	7 45	9 52				

Miles	Up.	Week Days.											
		mrn	mrn	mrn	aft	aft	aft	aft	aft				
	Hemel Hempsted ¶ dep.	7 22	8 32	11 48	2 38	5 20	6 38	8 20					
4¾	Redbourn	7 37	8 46	12 3	2 42	4 55	3 56	6 54	8 39				
8	Harpenden 576, 578 arr.	7 48	8 57	12 13	2 52	4 16	5 45	7 4	8 51				
32½	578 London (St. Pan.) ar	8 40	9 41	1 4	4 17	5 7	7 14		10 12				

March 1909

HARPENDEN and HEMEL HEMPSTED (3rd class only).—Midland.

	Down.	Week Days only.							Miles	Up.	Week Days only.							NOTES.
		mrn	mrn	mrn	aft	aft	aft	aft			mrn	mrn	aft	aft	aft	aft	aft	aft	
	642 London (St. Pancras) dep.	4 25	7 50	11 35	1 3	3 3	3 35	5 6	3 35	7 50		Heath Park Halt .... dep.	7 55	12 33				6 34		¶ Over 1¼ miles to Boxmoor and Hemel Hempstead (L. & N.W.) Station.
	Harpenden .... dep.		7 19	8 50	12 25	2 0	4 27	5 58	7 22	8 45		Hemel Hempsted ¶	6 35	8 0	6 28	3 3	2 30	5 0	6 40	8 0	
3¼	Redbourn ¶		7 28	9 0	12 35	2 8	10 4	3 76	8 7	32	8 55	5¾	Redbourn .... (644	6 51	8 16	22 2	3 54	3 46	5 17	6 56	8 16	
8	Hemel Hempsted ¶		7 44	9 15	12 51	2 26	4 52	6 24	7 47	9 10	8	Harpenden ** 353, 642, arr. 7 18	26 1	32 3	43 3	5 43	5 27	7 6	8 26	
8½	Heath Park Halt .... arr.		7 47		12 54	2 29		6 27			32½	644 London (St. Pancras) arr. 8 15	9 13	2 52	4 33	5 e 10	6 30	8 57	10 48	

s Except Sats. *s* Sats. only. ¶ "Halts" at Beaumont's and Godwin's, between Redbourn and Hemel Hempsted. ** About 1 mile to G. N. Station.

July 1922

HARPENDEN and HEMEL HEMPSTED (3rd class only).

Miles	Down.	Week Days only.					Miles	Up.	Week Days only.						NOTES.
		mrn	S	S	E				mrn	S	S	aft			A Over 1¼ mls to Hemel Hempsted and Boxmoor.
	682 London (St. Pancras) dep.	7 45	11 27	1 2	5 3			Heath Park Halt .... dep.	7 48	11 2	12 55	E			
	Harpenden .... dep.	8 43	12 32	2 14	5 47		½	Hemel Hempsted A	7 55	11 16	3 1	4 47			B About 1 mile to L. & N. E. Station.
1¾	Roundwood Halt	8 47	12 42	1 5	51		2	Godwin's Halt	7 58	21 3		4 51			
3¼	Redbourn	8 55	12 52	26 5	59		4½	Beaumont's Halt	8 41	21 8	11 4	58			
4¾	Beaumont's Halt	8 59	12 53	2 9	2		5½	Redbourn	8 9	31 3	153	5 4			E Except Sats.
6¼	Godwin's Halt	9 6	124 2	36 6	8		6¼	Roundwood Halt ..... (365	8 9	16 1	34 3	2 5 13			S Sats. only.
8	Hemel Hempsted A	9 10	12 6 2	4 6	13		8¾	Harpenden B 682, 684, arr. 8 20	1 42	32 3	2 5 17			
8½	Heath Park Halt .... arr.	9 13	124 2	43 6	16		32½	684 London (St. Pancras). arr. 9 10	2 39	4 34	6 38			

A Service of Omnibuses (L.P.T.B.) run between Harpenden, Redbourn and Hemel Hempsted and Boxmoor Stations.

March 1938

HARPENDEN, HEMEL HEMPSTED and HEATH PARK HALT (Third class only).

Miles	Down.	Week Days only.					Miles	Up.	Week Days only.				
		mrn		aft					mrn		aft		
	682 London (St. Pancras) .. dep.	7 25	..	4 30	..	..		Heath Park Halt .... dep.	7 28	..	4 37	..	..
	Harpenden .... dep.	8 43		5 35	..	..	2	Godwin's Halt	7 35		4 47	..	..
1¾	Roundwood Halt	8 47		5 39	..	..	4½	Beaumont's Halt	7 44		4 53	..	..
3¼	Redbourn	8 55		5 47	..	..	5½	Redbourn	7 49		5 1	..	..
4¾	Beaumont's Halt	8 59		5 50	..	..	6¼	Roundwood Halt	7 56		5 8	..	..
6¼	Godwin's Halt	9 6		5 57	..	..	8¾	Harpenden 682, 684, 854 arr.	8 0		5 14	..	..
8	Hemel Hempsted	9 10		6 1	..	..	32½	684 London (St. Pancras). arr.	9 0		6 48	..	..
8½	Heath Park Halt .... arr.	9 13		6 4	..	..							

E Except Saturdays
A Service of Omnibuses (L.P.T.B.) run between Harpenden, Redbourn and Hemel Hempsted and Boxmoor Stations.

February 1946

HARPENDEN

Station

Goods Shed

W.M

II. The 1898 survey shows the
location of both signal boxes (S.B.)

Institute

The Welcomes

D E N

1.   At the junction with Station Road stood the stationmasters house, built in 1870. On this particular day, Harpenden was holding its popular horse races and wagonettes queued to transport spectators to the course on the Common. The house was demolished on 24th September 1988 and offices were built on the site in 2005/6. (Authors coll.)

2.	A weighbridge hut and coal merchants offices were situated in the goods yard, east of the station. Building materials were also laid out here for sale. When the yard closed in 1964, this area became a car park. (Authors coll.)

3.	For many years, well respected William "Cabbie" Hogg operated his horse-drawn taxi service from the station. This postcard was issued in his retirement year, 1936. (Authors coll.)

4.   Freight trains for the Hemel Hempstead branch were assembled in the sidings in 1925. Just visible, behind the coalman and his horse, is a private owner coal wagon belonging to T.F.Poulter, coal merchant of Heath Park Depot. (Mrs R.Grey)

5.   This general view of the station, taken around 1912, provided a rare glimpse of Harpenden North signalbox, beyond the footbridge, which controlled the short bay, built in 1906 at the north end of the down fast platform for outgoing Hemel Hempstead branch trains only. (Lens of Sutton)

(Inset below).   Seen in the bay, soon after it was completed, is a 4-4-0T built by Hudswell, Clarke & Rogers. It is coupled to an ex-Pullman car, which was converted to push-pull working and was used on the branch for over 20 years.   (G.W.Goslin coll.)

6.   By the time this photograph was taken in 1935, the LMS was running both train and bus services between Harpenden and Boxmoor. A single coach was therefore sufficient for the few railway passengers. It is hauled by class 3F 0-6-0 no. 7248. (J.Jarvis)

7.   Harpenden Station signalbox was built by the LMS in 1933 on the down side of the main line and it took over the work of the former North and South signalboxes. (G.Woodward)

8.   An interior view of the signalbox features the 45 lever frame which controlled points and signals on the main line and to the sidings. The box closed on 20th October 1979 and was demolished in January 1980. (N.Payne)

9.   At the south end of the goods yard, the points into the siding from the up slow line were worked from a ground frame hut containing three levers. This was abolished in October 1976, when the line was being resignalled. (G.Woodward)

10.   Passengers passed through this doorway straight into the station booking hall, situated on the west side of the main line, at the top of an inclined approach road. The suffix "Central" was in use from 25th November 1950 to 18th April 1966. (A.Swain)

11.   The old footbridge was of metal construction, lined with wood boarding, and had a pitched roof above high level windows. The wooden steps were protected with metal treads. The smell of stale smoke and steam always pervaded the atmosphere in this box-like structure.
(Mrs S.Woodward)

12.   On a wintry day in the 1950s, class 4 0-6-0 no. 43888 laboured its way through the station with a train of coal wagons bound for Hemel Hempstead gasworks. (A.Turner)

13.   A special train, organised by the Locomotive Club of Great Britain, ran from Harpenden to Heath Park on 11th May 1957. Hauled by class 3F 0-6-0 no. 43245 (a regular locomotive on the branch), the empty train sets out from the down siding. (Authors coll.)

14.   The station canopy offered passengers shelter from the heavy rain as the LCGB special train approached the down fast platform. (Authors coll.)

15.   A correctly spelt "Nickey" headboard took pride of place on the buffer beam of class 3MT 2-6-2 no. 40026 for its South Beds Locomotive Club excursion to Hemel Hempstead on 24th September 1960. (Authors coll.)

Other views of this station and the branch can be found in *St. Albans to Bedford* **in picture nos 10-25.**

16.   The closure of Harpenden North signalbox on 2nd April 1933 resulted in the abandonment of the bay. Some time later it was filled in and a bicycle shed erected there. (G.Woodward)

NORTH OF HARPENDEN

17.   Looking south from Carlton Road footbridge, a young photographer tried out his camera on a train of empty wagons as it returned from Hemel Hempstead in 1936, in the process recording the only known view of the North signalbox from this direction. (A.Turner)

18.   From 1888, Hemel Hempstead branch trains ran to and from Harpenden Station, using the up and down fast tracks of the main line, in the foreground, which then ran north under the footbridge and on towards Harpenden Junction. This photograph is believed to date from the mid-1890s, soon after the line was quadrupled. (Authors coll.)

HARPENDEN JUNCTION

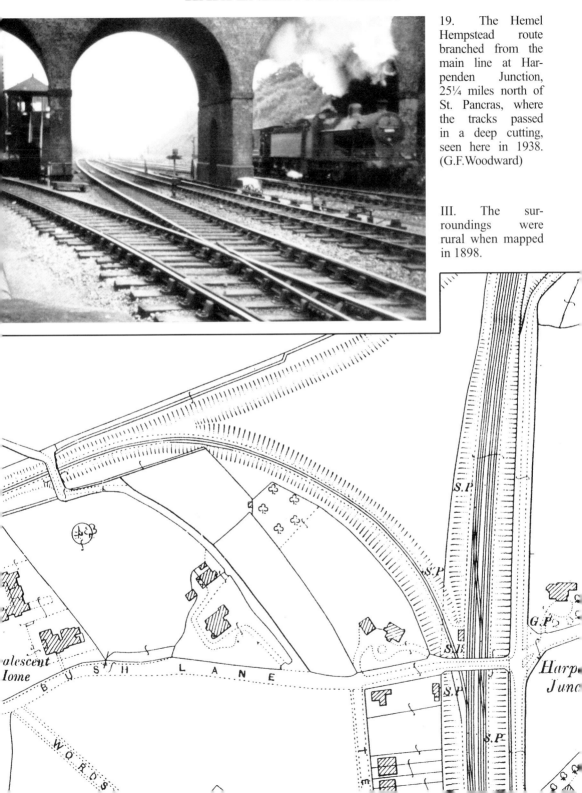

19. The Hemel Hempstead route branched from the main line at Harpenden Junction, 25¼ miles north of St. Pancras, where the tracks passed in a deep cutting, seen here in 1938. (G.F.Woodward)

III. The surroundings were rural when mapped in 1898.

20.   Removal of trees and scrub from the railway bank opposite the junction in 1972 allowed this previously unavailable view of Hollybush Lane bridge and the Hemel Hempstead line curving off behind the signalbox. The steps to the left of the bridge provided access for staff. (J.Heys)

21.   The photographer had to lean over the south parapet of Hollybush Lane bridge to catch no. 43245 as it propelled a brake van slowly onto the branch in April 1957. (J.Wood)

22.   Following closure of the branch, the points were clipped out of use on 1st July 1979. Removal of them, prior to replacement with plain track, was undertaken by this track gang on 21st March 1980. (G.Woodward)

23.   Type 2 diesel locomotive no. D5194, with its loaded wagons rounds the curve in June 1967. Lack of land for this Harpenden facing curve in 1888, meant that the bank needed a substantial retaining wall (seen through the arch). Signal lamps were tended in the corrugated iron hut. (R.Flanagan)

➡

24.   This junction signalbox replaced an earlier structure and opened in 1892. John Woodward (author's grandfather) joined the MR at Derby in 1890 but transferred here as a signalman, where he remained for 37 years, until his retirement in 1939. (G.F.Woodward)

➡

25.   Seen inside the signalbox in February 1952 is part of the MR lever frame. The signal wire adjusters are below the single line staff for the Hemel Hempstead branch which is in its cradle by the door. (A.Turner)

26.   Yet another signalbox was built to accommodate a larger lever frame. Seen here just prior to the changeover, the two signalboxes were so close together that staff could only access the new one by a ladder, as the steps could not be constructed until the old structure had been removed. (Authors coll.)

27.   The new signalbox, built to a BR(M) design, opened on Sunday 24th November 1957 and was fully in use by 8.0pm that day. To restock the coal bunker at the foot of the steps, a wagon was shunted onto the branch, from which coal was barrowed. (G.Woodward)

28.   Experienced signalman, Alf Morgan, worked in both the old and new signalboxes. In between trains, he devoted much time to helping his trainee signalman learn the job. The signalbox diagram over the block shelf clearly showed the line to Hemel Hempstead leaving the main line. (G.Woodward)

29.   This shabby 4F drifted slowly round
the curve in July 1961 with an evening goods
train from Hemel Hempstead, made up of vans
carrying paperware from the John Dickinson
factory at Apsley, while the signalman waited
to collect the single line staff from the fireman.
(G.Woodward)

→

30.   The signalbox became redundant on
20th October 1979 due to resignalling, prior to
electrification of the main line. The wooden top
section was soon removed for reuse elsewhere,
but it was another year before the brick base was
demolished. (Mrs S.Woodward)

→

31.   An aerial view of the National Childrens Home in 1930 shows the course of the original
curve that gave Hemel Hempstead trains access to the main line, by way of a junction half a mile
north of Hollybush Lane bridge. (Authors coll.)

32.   Another section of retaining wall was needed at the western extremity of the 1888 curve from the junction and a check rail was installed because of its sharp radius. The trees on the left have grown in the former north curve cutting. (G.Woodward)

MIDLAND RAILWAY.   This Ticket is issued subject to the Regulations & Conditions stated in the Company's Time Tables & Bills.

THIRD CLASS.   THIRD CLASS.
AVAILABLE ON DAY OF ISSUE ONLY.

REDBOURN to

HARPENDEN

FARE 3½d.   FARE 3½d.
Redbourn-Harpenden   Redbourn-Harpenden

4270   4270

WEST OF
HARPENDEN JUNCTION

33.   On a frosty morning in 1960, class 4 2-6-0 no. 43120 approached the Ambrose Lane bridge with a train of empty vans, having built up a good head of steam for the steep gradient ahead. (G.Woodward)

34.   This impressive 66 feet wide, four arched brick bridge spanned the cutting and, being the first on the branch, at one time carried a MR no. 1 bridgeplate. After the track was taken up, the old trackbed was adopted by the local authority and designated a cycleway and footpath known as The Nicky Way (recently corrected to Nickey Way). These access steps were created in 1985. (Authors coll.)

35. When the line was leased by Hemelite, their limit of working was just west of the bridge. BR locomotives shunted wagons, loaded with fly ash, to that point during the night, much to the annoyance of local residents. These were collected by a Hemelite locomotive as and when required and empty wagons returned. (L.Casey)

36. Hemel Hempstead Model Railway Society arranged a round tour on 25th September 1960, going out over the branch and eventually returning to the town by way of the main line at Hemel Hempstead & Boxmoor station. A four car DMU was used for the trip, seen here passing the outer home signal. (G.Woodward)

37   Known locally as The Arch, this bridge had an embankment built over the top to raise the level of the track, thus reducing the incline. Being at an angle to the road (A1081) resulted in a very narrow pathway to one side. The advertising hoardings were erected in 1935. (G.Woodward)

38.　　Harpenden Home Guard and Civil Defence held a combined exercise on the bridge in November 1942, during which American bombers flew over, adding realism to the event! The role of the Home Guard was to protect the bridge, while being watched by a team of observers. (E.Brandreth)

ROUNDWOOD HALT

39.   The small unmanned Roundwood Halt, viewed from the footbridge in 1938, had a prefabricated concrete platform front and carried one LMS Hawkseye nameboard. Passengers waited in the little wooden shelter. The halt came into use on 8th August 1927. (D.Barrie)

L. M. & S. R.
FOR CONDITIONS SEE BACK
FARE 2½d.
ROUNDWOOD HALT &
HARPENDEN
4326

40. Hemel Hempstead bound 43245 ascends the 1 in 37 incline from Luton Road bridge with one wagon and a brakevan in 1950. (Transport Treasury)

41. The old wooden footbridge which had served Roundwood Halt was replaced by a tubular steel bridge on 26th September 1951. This remained until 25th February 1984, when it was dismantled and a path laid over the former trackbed. The short telegraph pole had allowed wires to pass under the bridge. (Authors coll.)

42.   A train of vans, hauled by class 4F 2-6-0 no. 43119, returns from Hemel Hempstead, past the fixed distant signal for the junction, heading east through the former Halt in August 1962. By this time, fields in the area had given way to extensive housing development. (G.Woodward)

43.   The Hemelite Drewry diesel shunter, no. D2203, propelling several empty wagons back to the changeover point at Ambrose Lane, slowly rumbled its way through the heavily overgrown Halt in September 1971. (J.Heys)

44.   A little further west, the line crossed an ancient trackway to Redbourn, which became known as Townsend Lane crossing. It merely comprised old sleepers laid between and beside the rails and, although the gates survived for many years, they were not used in recent times. (Authors coll.)

45. The rural charm of this railway was captured here as it passed through Knott Wood, on a 1 in 39 gradient down into the River Ver valley at Redbourn. Local people used this stretch of line as a footpath to admire the violets, primroses, bluebells, palm and other flowering trees and also to look for glow-worms and hear nightingales sing. (Authors coll.)

46. As the gradient eased to 1 in 304, Hemelite locomotive no. D2207 with its ash wagons passes over a crossing used by Rothamsted Experimental Station staff to gain access to their fields on both sides of the line. (J.Heys)

NORTH OF REDBOURN

47.   This postcard, featuring the River Ver dating from about 1912, depicted a very rural scene as the railway crossed Harpenden Lane on a well maintained embankment and a low plate girder bridge. After the line closed the bridge was removed and all this area was incorporated into the Redbourn Bypass scheme. (Authors coll.)

48.   The bridge had just been reopened following repairs after a lorry collided with it, when no. D2207, running light engine, passed over it on 28th April 1972. After three similar accidents that year, black and yellow hazard stripes were painted on it. (J.Heys)

REDBOURN

49.   As a cost-cutting experiment, the LMS commissioned Karrier Motors to build a vehicle which could be run on roads and rails. On 22nd January 1931 it was demonstrated on the branch for the benefit of LMS officials, invited guests and the press, who had travelled from London to Redbourn in a special train hauled by 4-4-0 no. 556. (A.Tozer)

50.   The 26-seater Ro-Railer coach carried out three trial runs, using a board ramp, which had been specially constructed in a siding beside the goods shed, to transfer from rail to road. (A.Tozer)

51.   Staff had been trained to effect the changeover from rail to road wheels, a process which took less than four minutes. This close-up of the mechanism also recorded the presence of inside-keyed track in the siding. (A.Tozer)

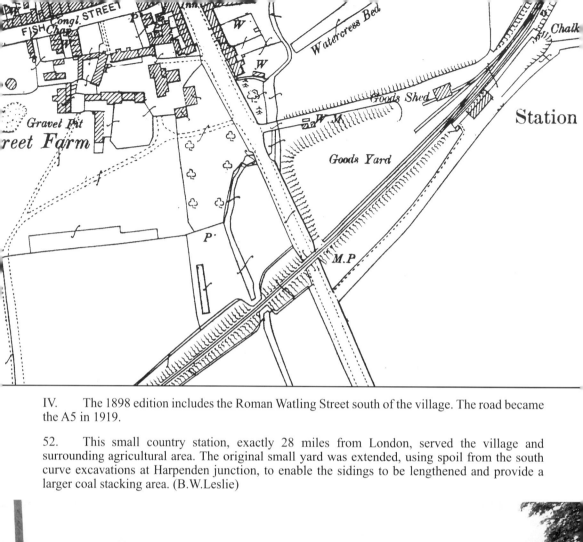

IV.   The 1898 edition includes the Roman Watling Street south of the village. The road became the A5 in 1919.

52.   This small country station, exactly 28 miles from London, served the village and surrounding agricultural area. The original small yard was extended, using spoil from the south curve excavations at Harpenden junction, to enable the sidings to be lengthened and provide a larger coal stacking area. (B.W.Leslie)

53.   In heavy rain, class 4F no. 43119 arrived with the afternoon Hemel Hempstead train on 22nd August 1958. The village grew from 1932 souls in 1901 to 3835 in 1961. (C.Polkinghorne)

54.   Looking from the goods yard, in an easterly direction, the station had been without passengers for several years and was beginning to show signs of neglect in August 1958. (B.W.Leslie)

55.   A newspaper advertisement appeared in the Railway Times on 19th June 1875 inviting tenders for the construction of stations, together with other works to complete the new railway. Work started soon after on the wooden buildings. The small white building at the end of the platform was a platelayers hut. (R.Flanagan)

56.   Following severance of the branch and therefore Hemelites inability to use rail transport, locomotive D2203 was sold for preservation and made its last journey to Redbourn on 7th February 1982. As the whole BR network was closed by strike action, this could have been the only rail movement that day! (R.Marshall)

57.   The A5 bridge was redecked on 1st July 1895, but in 1930 the road was lowered to enable early open topped double decker buses to pass beneath it, but even then passengers had to duck their heads! When covered double deckers were introduced in 1951, both this and the River Ver bridge (left) had to be raised by two feet and a short section of track was relaid. (G.Woodward)

58.   Several enthusiasts specials were organised by Hemelite, usually aboard empty coal wagons - until BR banned them. Not to be beaten, the LCGB ran two trips on 17th October 1970, with participants travelling in the cab and standing on the running board of D2207, witnessed as it crossed the Watling Street bridge. (D.Andrews)

WEST OF REDBOURN

59.   Connors Crossing, by the 28¼ milepost, was the scene of several accidents. More than
once local residents campaigned for a footbridge. Ballast for the original railway was dug from
the field on the left, for which a siding was laid. (G.Woodward)

60.   In 1895 Chequers Lane bridge was rebuilt using a new deck made by the Consett Iron &
Steel Company. New timber supports for the rails and new fixing plates were put in and the track
reballasted in 1952. (R.E.Lacy)

BEAUMONT'S HALT

61.   This halt took its name from a local tenant farmer who had left the area many years earlier and it opened on 9th August 1905. It was preceded by the only gated level crossing on the branch, for which the MR built a gatekeepers house. Oil lamps on the gates and platform were tended by staff from Redbourn station and extinguished by the guard of the last train. (B.W.Leslie)

L M. & S. R

FOR CONDITIONS SEE BACK

(UP)

FARE 2½d.

HARPENDEN AND
ROUNDWOOD HALT

1691

1691

62.   The level crossing gates were protected by a distant signal in each direction operated by the crossing keeper, but even so there were occasions when locomotives collided with the gates. (B.W.Leslie)

63.   In latter days, the signals were fixed at caution and the crossing keepers post was abolished, leaving train staff to open and shut the gates. (Transport Treasury)

64. The platform reflected the economies of the MR, being built of old sleepers. Although virtually derelict by August 1958, the LMS nameboard survived intact. In the background, M1 Motorway construction was well advanced, including a bridge over the branch, wide enough to allow for double track. (B.W.Leslie)

65. With signs of autumn all around, the 4-car DMU used for the Hemel Hempstead Model Railway Society outing on 25th September 1960 passed the halt. (K.Taylor)

66. From a brakevan, looking back towards Beaumont's Halt, the twisting course of the branch was evident as it passed beneath the motorway in 1967. (Transport Treasury)

67.   A little further on stood the fixed distant signal for Beaumont's Halt crossing and a prefabricated concrete fogmans hut; Sunnyside Crossing is in the foreground.
(Transport Treasury)

68.   At Wood End, the gradient of this straight section of track eased beyond the bridge, from 1 in 42 to 1 in 56, as far as Claydale Sidings. Although few people lived in this neighbourhood, a halt was considered in 1905, when the other halts were provided.
(G.Woodward)

69.   This two arch bridge was built with brick-saving recesses in the main walls and carried a MR no. 7 bridgeplate, fixed over a previously painted number. (R.E.Lacy)

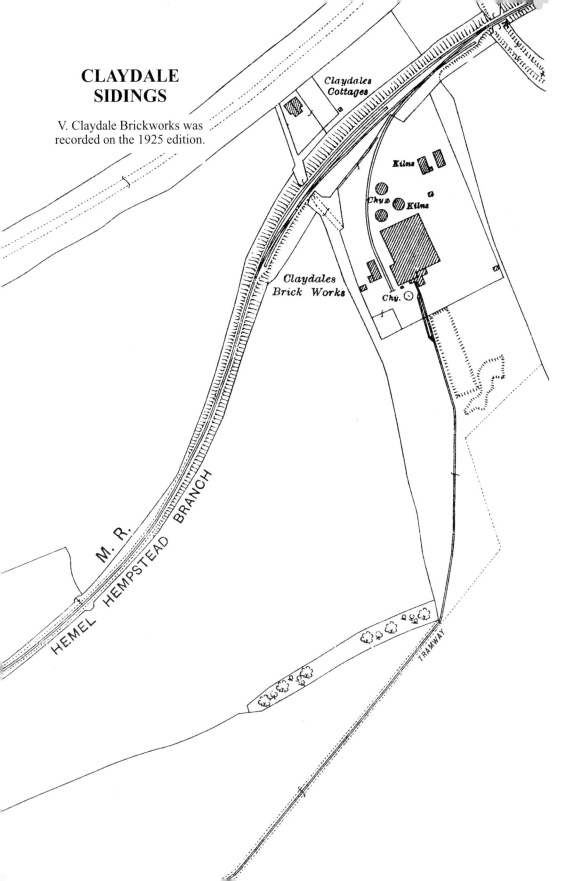

CLAYDALE
SIDINGS

V. Claydale Brickworks was
recorded on the 1925 edition.

Claydales
Cottages

Kilns

Chy.   Kilns

Claydales
Brick Works

Chy.

M. R.

HEMEL HEMPSTEAD BRANCH

TRAMWAY

70.   At the top of the gradient, the track levelled off and Claydale sidings ran into the brickworks. The point lever is seen on the right, in 1966. In the centre foreground was a lock, which had to be released, using the end of the single line staff, before the points could be operated. The points had to be returned to their normal position before the staff could be retrieved. (G. Woodward)

71.   This train of wagons, delivered direct to the works by BR, occupied the branch line. Here, the brake van was being uncoupled. (Transport Treasury)

72.   Full wagons were collected, one by one, unloaded and returned to a siding. In this general view on 16th May 1978, Hemelite's own Drewry diesel shunter stood alongside their 0-4-0 Simplex shunter. (G.Woodward)

73.   By 1964 the line terminated at the works of the Hemel Hempstead Lightweight Concrete Co. Ltd., who became the sole user of the branch. To satisfy the increased demand for their building blocks the works were considerably extended. (G.Woodward)

74.   At the end of the sidings, close to the older part of the works, was a wagon tippler, shown in use in August 1968. Having tilted the wagon, ash dropped out of the end door, down to a conveyor belt for transmission to a storage area or direct to the manufacturing plant. (J.Heys)

GODWIN'S HALT

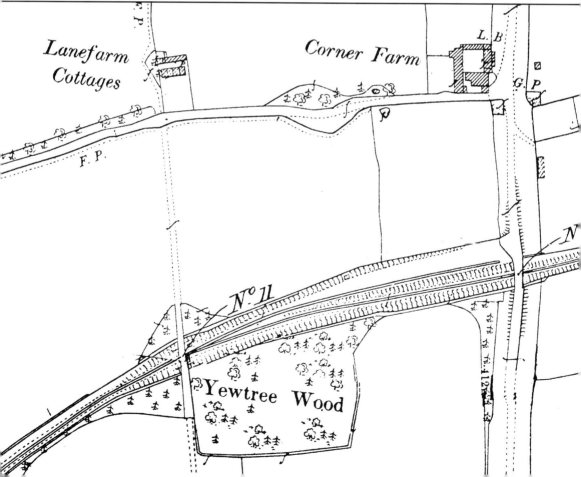

←———— 75.   In 1869 compulsory purchase orders were served on Shadrach Godwin of Grove Hill, to acquire land for the railway. He demanded an inflated price which resulted in protracted negotiations, during which he anticipated noise and annoyance from the trains, but in the end he requested a siding for his own use. (Authors coll.)

←———— VI.   Godwins Siding was recorded on the 1898 map. The halt was built west of bridge no. 11, north of the line.

76.   This halt, constructed of sleepers with a cinder surface, was opened on 9th August 1905 to serve the Cupid Green community. In 1907 a Pagoda shelter was erected on the platform, made from a material similar to corrugated iron. By 1958 nature was reclaiming the lineside but the soot stained footbridge remained with a platelayers hut below. The siding closed on 2nd March 1964. (B.W.Leslie)

WEST OF GODWIN'S HALT

77.   Here is another idyllic country scene, the backdrop being provided by the second largest construction on the railway. No more than a lane in this picture, the road was up-graded with the coming of Hemel Hempstead New Town and renamed Queensway. Footpath tunnels were bored through the massive embankment in 1958. (K.Whiteley)

78.   Passenger trains on the branch in the early 1900s were seldom photographed, so, although lacking in quality, this print from an old postcard is included as a rare record of a MR tank engine, with its two-coach train, on the neat embankment about a quarter of a mile south-west of the bridge. (A.Edwards)

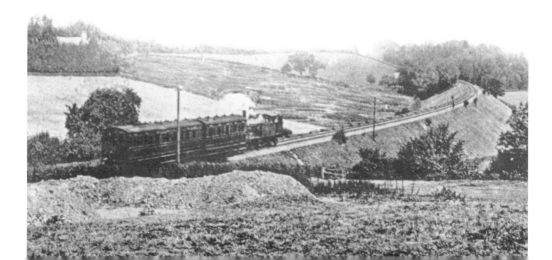

NORTH OF HEMEL HEMPSTEAD

79.   Adeyfield Road crossed the bridge which was situated immediately at the north end of Hemel Hempstead station platform. Some clue as to the date of this illustration can be gained from the presence of the MR slotted post signal, which was removed on 6th April 1887. (Authors coll.)

80.   A large crowd assembled on the bridge to witness a special event on the railway (thought to be the coming of the new railmotor). The Midland Hotel, on the far side of the railway, changed its name to The Mayflower after closure of the branch, but reverted to its old name in November 1998. (Hemel Hempstead Local History Society)

81.	The MR had two steam railmotors, nos 2233 and 2234, and one of these went into service, in conjunction with ordinary trains, on 1st October 1905. The railmotor was not powerful enough for the line's steep gradients and soon left the branch. (Authors coll.)

82.	The sparse interior of the railmotor, with wooden seating, afforded little comfort compared with that offered by the old Pullman coach then used on some of the branch trains. The compartment was lit by gas and notices requested passengers not to smoke. (Authors coll.)

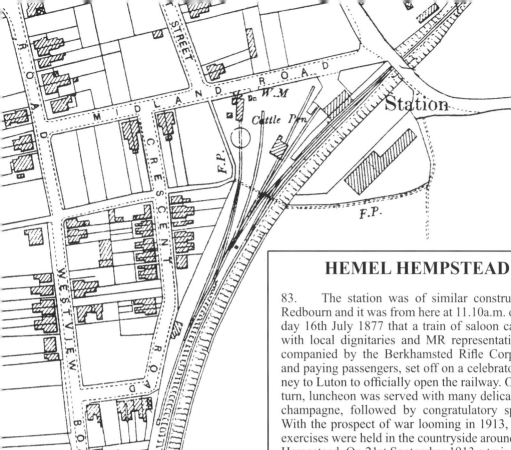

VII.   1898 edition.

HEMEL HEMPSTEAD

83.   The station was of similar construction to Redbourn and it was from here at 11.10a.m. on Monday 16th July 1877 that a train of saloon carriages, with local dignitaries and MR representatives, accompanied by the Berkhamsted Rifle Corps Band and paying passengers, set off on a celebratory journey to Luton to officially open the railway. On its return, luncheon was served with many delicacies and champagne, followed by congratulatory speeches. With the prospect of war looming in 1913, military exercises were held in the countryside around Hemel Hempstead. On 21st September 1913 a train arrived, loaded with siege guns, which were unloaded by a detachment of the Royal Garrison Artillery. Note, the station garden looked to be productive in vegetables. (Hemel Hempstead Local History Society)

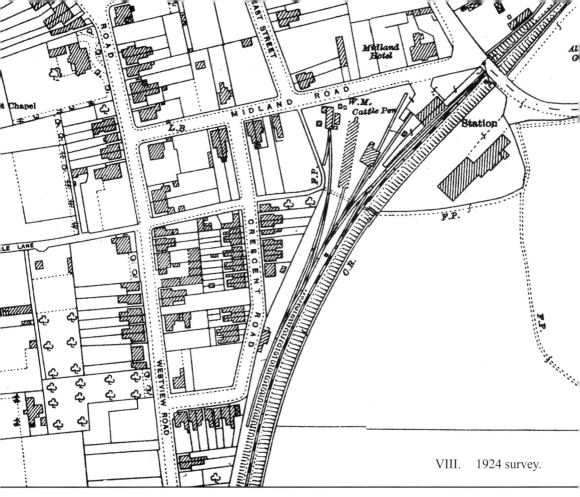

VIII.   1924 survey.

84.   Outside the station, the road had been closed to allow the equipment to be formed into horse drawn gun carriage teams, seen here beside the engine shed and water tower. (Hemel Hempstead Local History Society)

85.   A northward view from October 1929 emphasises the gradient. (H.C.Casserley)

86.   Class 4F 2-6-0 no. 43119 has brought its train of coal wagons to a halt in the station, to await shunting instructions, on l0th March 1956. (B.Connell)

87.   The locomotive of the LCGB special train awaits the return of its passengers on 11th May 1957, prior to tackling the demanding 1 in 39 gradient, which started immediately the other side of Adeyfield Road bridge. (S.Summerson)

88.   By July 1958 the condition of the track was causing concern and so a speed limit was imposed on the small number of freight trains which still used the line, as indicated by the illuminated sign on the platform. (B.W.Leslie)

89.   Fifteen years after passengers stopped using the station, the buildings were still in good order, though stripped of signs and notices. In May 1962, a locomotive crew had plenty of time for a chat during the slow process of taking water. The hydrant in the station platform was installed in 1905 for the railmotor. (S.Summerson)

90.   Once through the station, points beside the 32½ milepost led into the goods area, with sidings behind and west of the station buildings. They were formerly illuminated by tall gas lamps. On this occasion, locomotive class 4 2-6-0 no. 43121 steamed into the station with vans destined for the Dickinson paper traffic. (Authors coll.)

91.   The vans were shunted out of the station and, when needed, taken to the covered siding in the centre of the yard for loading. (A.Edwards)

92.   Originally the engine shed stood on this site and the upturned sleeper marked the end of the track which ran through it. A turntable was installed here on the insistence of the Board of Trade inspector before he would sanction the opening of the branch, but when an engine fell through it in 1897 it was not repaired, and subsequently removed. (Authors coll.)

93.   This MR hand-operated crane, dating from 1885, survived in the goods yard until about 1960. (S.Summerson)

Working timetable for September 1957 to June 1958.

ST. ALBANS TRIP ENGINE.

No. 87.			No. 87—*continued.*		
Class 4F (2-6-0) Engine.					
8.35 a.m. to 8.30 p.m. (SX.), 2.15 p.m. (SO.).				arr.	dep.
	arr.	dep.		P.M.	P.M.
	a.m.	a.m.	Harpenden	......	2 33 SX.
St Albans Loco. Shed...	......	8 35 LE.	Redbourn ...	2 48	3 13 SX.
Harpenden ...	8 50	9 45	Godwin's Halt...	3 25	3 50 SX.
Redbourn ...	9 58	10 13	Hemel Hempstead ...	3 57	4 18 SX.
Godwin's Halt	10*26	10*28	Heath Park ...	4 25	4 30 SX.
Hemel Hempstead ...	10 35	10 55	Gas Works Sdgs.	4 37	5 5 SX.
Heath Park ...	11 2	11 7	Hemel Hempstead ...	5 15	6 5 SX.
Gas Works Sdgs.	11 13	11 40	Redbourn ...	6 30	6 45 SX.
		P.M.	Harpenden ...	7 7	8 7 SX.
Heath Park ...	11 47	12 35	St. Albans ...	8 20	......
	P.M.		Detach, attach or Shunt at Godwin Sdgs.		
Hemel Hempstead	12 42	1 10	or Station Yards as required.		
Redbourn ...	1 35	1 50	Work as required.		
Harpenden ...	2 5	2 15 LE.(cpld.	St. Alban s		8 30 LE. SX.
St. Albans ...	2 30	...... SO.).	St. Albans Loco. Shed		......
Continued in next column.					

94.   Looking south from the end of the station platform, class 4 no. 43118 has assembled its train and awaited departure. The lever frame beside the locomotive controlled the points for the passing loop and those into the sidings. (S.Summerson)

SOUTH OF HEMEL HEMPSTEAD

95.　　From the station the line dropped down a 1 in 51 gradient under Hillfield Road bridge, evident in the distance. The chalk on the bank and track marked an unauthorised short cut footpath across the line. Class 4 no. 43031 was just visible on the headshunt in the goods yard on 28th July 1956. (S.Summerson)

96.　　With three wide arches, Marlowes Viaduct was the largest structure on the line. It was built slightly curved and took account of the descending gradient in the direction of Heath Park. Demolition took place on 2nd July 1960. In 1957 Marlowes was converted to dual carriageway, as the main street in the new town, by using the central arch for the second carriageway and a footpath was created on a plinth overhanging the River Gade in the third archway. (A.Willmott)

97.　　A train of empty coal wagons hauled by class 4 no. 43119 crosses the viaduct on 10th March 1956. Although the embankment was neat, with trees trimmed, the track was obviously receiving little maintenance. (B.Connell)

98.   Using this aerial photograph, the branch could be traced from Hemel Hempstead station and goods yard (in the top right corner), down the gradient through an area known as Paradise and across the viaduct to Heath Park (lower left). A section of the original line left The Moor here and ran north, parallel with the road, for a short distance. (Commission for New Towns)

HEATH PARK
HALT

99.   In recognition of the efforts made by the people of Hemel Hempstead during World War I, a captured 27 ton German tank was given to the town. Being too heavy for local road bridges, it was delivered by rail to Heath Park Depot. Having been driven to a prepared plinth near Heath Park Halt, a handing over ceremony was held on 21st February 1920. (3rd Boxmoor Boy Scouts)

100.   The lamp behind the crowd in the previous illustration was added to a drinking fountain made by local ironfounders, Cranstones, in 1835. It was sited near Heath Park Hotel, close to the Halt and Corner Hall Road. The HH&LNWRCo. intended to build a cattle arch here, but the local Highways Committee insisted on a proper bridge so as not to have to deviate the road. (A.Willmott)

101.   This embankment was built as part of the original line but just south of Station Road bridge the extended line branched off north-east and on 9th August 1905 a halt was opened here. During passage of a military convoy in 1944, the deck of this bridge was removed by a Sherman tank on a transporter. (A.Willmott)

102.   The Halt occupied an elevated situation between Station Road bridge and bridge no. 21, where branch passenger services ultimately terminated. At the far end of the platform were the points for Heath Park Goods Depot sidings, seen in 1958. (B.W.Leslie)

HEATH PARK GOODS DEPOT

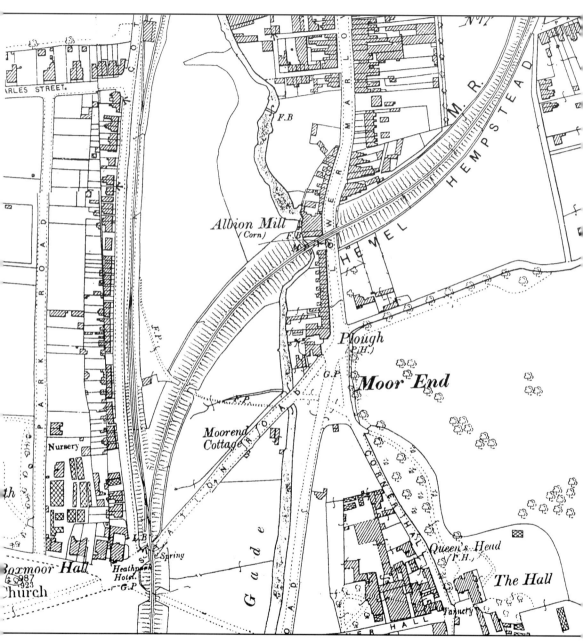

IX. The halt was built between the two bridges lower left.

103.   The Depot was situated beside Cotterells Road and was sometimes referred to simply as
Cotterells Sidings. This general view in 1936 shows a cluster of buildings, including a goods shed
and coal merchants offices. A weighbridge was sited just inside the gates. (Authors coll.)

104.   On 13th September 1949 several wagons were derailed on the approach to the Depot. A breakdown train arrived, hauled by 0-6-0 no. 3806, still bearing its LMS letters, as was the staff van. (A.Willmott)

105.   One of these wagons, which had run away during shunting, was retrieved by the Cricklewood steam crane, an operation witnessed by a large crowd of schoolchildren. (B.Berlanny)

106.   With the brake van left at Heath Park, locomotive no. 43119 carried out wagon shunting operations in the Depot sidings and, having formed its train, took up a position on the passing loop on 10th March 1956. (B.Connell)

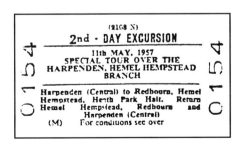

(2168 N)
2nd · DAY EXCURSION
11th MAY, 1957
SPECIAL TOUR OVER THE
HARPENDEN, HEMEL HEMPSTEAD
BRANCH

Harpenden (Central) to Redbourn, Hemel
Hempstead, Heath Park Halt. Return
Hemel Hempstead, Redbourn and
Harpenden (Central)
(M)   For conditions see over

0154   0154

107.   On arrival at Heath Park Halt, the 1957 LCGB special train reversed into the Depot with the guard clinging on to the outside of a carriage. Some of the passengers had alighted to watch the locomotive run round its train. (Authors coll.)

108.   With the run round complete, the LCGB locomotive propelled its carriages back to the platform at Heath Park Halt for another photo call, where passengers rejoined their train, putting their trust in the rickety handrail on Station Road bridge. This was the last passenger train to use the section of line below Hemel Hempstead station. (A.Turner)

109.   The crew of 0-6-0 no. 43246 appeared to have stopped their train of private owner coal wagons on Corner Hall Road bridge specially for the camera in 1948. Although the locomotive displayed its BR number, the tender still carried its LMS lettering. It would appear that cows were still allowed to graze The Moor at this time. (A.Willmott)

110.   The bridge was of girder construction with brick abutments and carried painted low bridge warnings. Above the deck corrugated iron sheeting prevented cinders from locomotives falling onto the road below. A well worn unofficial footpath approached the Halt up the embankment. (Authors coll.)

1	L.M.S. RAILWAY AND LONDON TRANSPORT	7
	WEEKLY TICKET.	
2	*No.* **3852**	8
3	AVAILABLE FOR 12 SINGLE JOURNEYS BETWEEN **REDBOURN** AND	9
4	**HARPENDEN** By L. T. BUS (also valid by Rail)	10
5	*Date of* } Expiry } .... The Holder of this Season Ticket is not guaranteed a seat in any particular bus.	11
6	*Name of* } Holder } .... [TURN OVER.	12

111.   South of Corner Hall Road bridge the line passed over an area of common land, by way of an embankment lined with horse chestnut trees. Just past the bridge a catch point was put in as a safety measure, should any wagons run away from the gasworks sidings further on. (B.W.Leslie)

112.   The line was carried over the Grand Junction Canal (later Grand Union) just below Boxmoor Lock, by means of a plate girder bridge which was rebuilt in 1896 using new girders under the rails and secondhand ones on the outside. (Authors coll.)

113.   The embankment continued on the far side of the canal, as far as the A41 London Road bridge, where on 10th March 1956 locomotive no. 43119 was making its way to the gasworks. (B.Connell)

→

114.   Even before the first Act of Parliament was passed, the HH&LNWRCo. were hopeful of getting permission to reduce road levels so they could suffice with lower embankments, but this proposal was rejected. In consequence, London Road bridge did not have the clearance needed by modern day traffic and on occasions tall vehicles struck it. (Authors coll.)

→

115.   This panoramic view shows the course of the line as it crossed The Moor, from its junction with Heath Park sidings, over the canal and River Bulbourne to London Road. When the line opened in 1877 it was recorded that all the section below Hemel Hempstead station was overgrown and unused, but here the track is neat and useable. Because the MR started taking coal to the gasworks (just out of the picture) in 1880 this photograph could have been taken soon after. (R.Hands)

BOXMOOR

X. This 1898 extract shows the southern limit of the
branch and its proximity to the quadruple track of the LNWR.

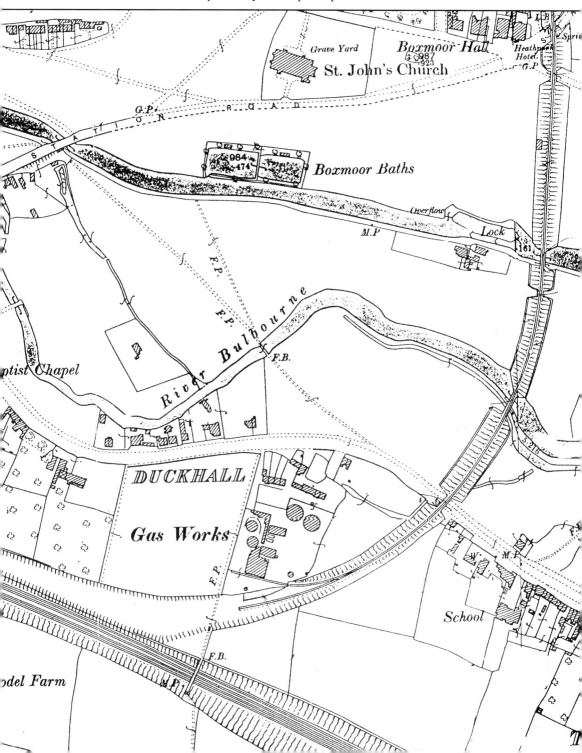

116.   Boxmoor Gasworks started small and gradually expanded to dominate the landscape. Because of the sites close proximity to the line, the MR agreed to construct a siding into the works to replace the horse and cart deliveries from Hemel Hempstead station. (Authors coll.)

117.   For most of its existence, this was where the Hemel Hempstead branch terminated, 33 miles and 59 chains from London. The lefthand track was the remains of an original unused section of railway and the righthand track was the gasworks siding. A second siding was built later, giving capacity for 26 wagons. (B.W.Leslie)

118.   Because of the proposed development of the New Town, the line was closed between Hemel Hempstead station and the A41 bridge. To enable the gasworks to continue receiving coal, a siding was laid to it from Boxmoor goods yard. The line opened on 31st August 1959, but the gasworks closed on 1st April 1960. The redundant length of track (furthest from the camera in this picture) remained in use as a siding. (Transport Treasury)

**The main line station is
featured in the
Watford to Leighton Buzzard album.**

119.   Viewed from the same bridge, but 14 years later, the sidings have all but disappeared and the course of the Hemel Hempstead railway is just defined by a gap in the trees. According to a plan dated 1869, this was where the branch would have joined the LNWR main line if agreement had been reached between the two companies. (G.Woodward)

120.   Although the 1869 proposal came to nothing, on 21st October that year the LNWR finally agreed a connection from the new HH&LNWR line, which had been built as far as this bridge. An additional wide arch, of totally different style, was therefore added to Roughdown Road bridge and track laid through it into the goods yard, where a turntable connection with LNWR sidings was installed. Its use, though, has always been in doubt. This view in 1938 shows a later siding from the main line. (D.Barrie)

MIDLAND RAILWAY

HORTICULTURAL SHOW
AT HARPENDEN.

On Wednesday, Aug. 26,

Cheap Excursion Tickets will be issued to

HARPENDEN

FROM

LUTON AND ST. ALBANS

By any ORDINARY TRAIN, and from LUTON only by SPECIAL TRAIN at 4.0 p.m.

The Tickets will be available for return on the day of issue only, by any ordinary train (except the 9.12 p.m. from HARPENDEN to LUTON), or by SPECIAL TRAIN leaving HARPENDEN at 9.0 p.m. for LUTON, and at 9.55 p.m. for ST. ALBANS.

FARES THERE AND BACK—THIRD CLASS.

8d.

Children under 3 years of age, Free; above 3 and under 12, Half-Fare. The Tickets are not transferable. No Luggage allowed.

First and Third Class RETURN TICKETS at a Single Fare-and-a-Quarter for the Double Journey, will be issued to HARPENDEN from BEDFORD and intermediate Stations to LEAGRAVE inclusive, from HEMEL HEMPSTED, and from HENDON and intermediate Stations to RADLETT inclusive.

The Tickets will be available for returning on the day of issue only.

Derby, Aug., 1896. GEO. H. TURNER, General Manager.

Bemrose & Sons, Limited, Printers, Derby; and London.

Cheap Return Tickets
DAILY
TO AND FROM
ALL STATIONS
BETWEEN

Moorgate	St. Pancras	Barking
East Ham	St. Albans	Hemel Hempsted
	Luton Bedford	

AND INTERMEDIATE STATIONS

AVAILABILITY OF TICKETS.

OUTWARD—Weekdays—By any train except the following :
- 7.25 a.m., Bedford to St. Pancras.
- 7.57 a.m., Luton to St. Pancras.
- 8.10 a.m., Harpenden to St. Pancras.

Sunday—By any train (where train service exists).

RETURN—By any train on day of issue of ticket.

FIRST CLASS CHEAP TICKETS ARE ISSUED AT APPROXIMATELY 50% OVER TH THIRD CLASS FARE (fractions of a penny reckoned as a penny).

Passengers will be allowed to alight on the outward journey at a Station short of their destination or surrender of the outward half of their ticket, and on the return may commence their journey at an intermediate station or complete it at a Station short of the destination shown on the ticket.

CHILDREN under three years of age, free; three years and under fourteen, half-fares.

CONDITIONS OF ISSUE.

Day, Half-day and Evening Tickets are issued subject to the conditions applicable to tickets of thes descriptions as shewn in the Company's Time Tables.

For LUGGAGE ALLOWANCES also see Time Tables.

TICKETS ISSUED IN ADVANCE AT THE STATIONS AND AGENCIES.

Further Information may be obtained on application to any L M S Station, Office or Agency or to H. ROBERTS, District Passenger Manager, Euston Station, London, N.W.I. (Telephone EUSTON 123-

Oct., 1937. ASHTON DAVIES, Chief Commercial Manager
(E.R.O. 53360/1)

For EXCURSIONS from AMPTHILL, LUT

LONDON
(ST. PANCRAS STATION),
COOK'S EXCURSION TICKETS will be issued as under :—

FROM	Times of starting.				Return Fares to LONDON (St. Pancras)—Third Class.		RETURN ARRANGEMENTS.
	Aug. 4 h only. a.m.	All Dates, Day tr in. a.m.	a.m.	August 4th only. Half-day train. p.m.	Day Trip. s. d.	Half-day Trip. s. d.	Passengers return from St. Pancras on day of issue only, by any ordinary train after 4.0 p.m. (except 5.40 and 8.40 p.m.).
ST. ALBANS dep.	8 48	9*20	10 27	1 35 *August 4th excepted.	2 1	2 1	

On EVERY WEDNESDAY and SATURDAY
To LONDON For DAY & HALF-DAY
(ST. PANCRAS STATION),
EXCURSION TICKETS will be issued as under :—

FROM	Times of starting.				Return Fare to LONDON (St. Pancras). Third Class.	RETURN ARRANGEMENTS.
	A.M.	A.M.	P.M.	P.M.		The Return Trains will leave each day as under :—
HEMEL HEMPSTED ... at	8 33	11 52	2 28	3 43	2/9	From St. Pancras at 4.0 p.m., 4.45 p.m., 5.33 p.m. & 8.40 p.m. From Kentish Town at 4.50 p.m. and 8.39 p.m.
REDBOURN	8 47	12 7	2 42	3 57		
LONDON (St. Pancras) ... arr.	9 50	1 8	4 15	5 5		

CONDITIONS OF ISSUE OF TICKETS.

CHILDREN under three years of age free; three years and under twelve, half-fares.
NOTICE.—The tickets are not transferable, and will be available only on the dates, by the trains, and at the stations named; if used on any other date, by any other train, or at any other station than those named, the tickets will be forfeited and the full ordinary fare charged.
The Company gives notice that tickets for these excursions are issued at a reduced rate, and subject to the condition that the Company shall not be liable for any loss, damage, injury, or delay to passengers, arising from any cause whatsoever. No luggage allowed.

TICKETS, BILLS and all particulars may be obtained at the
MIDLAND RAILWAY CO.'S BOOKING OFFICES AND STATIONS
And at the Midland and L. & N.W. Co.'s Joint Office, 16, High Street, ST. ALBANS.

Derby, June, 1913.
B. 309/13. Bh.

W. GUY GRANET, General Manager.

Thos. Cook & Son, Printers, &c., L igate Ci us, London. (9357)

BRITISH RAILWAYS (E)   (S.T. H1779)
The Rly Correspondence & Travel Society
2nd NORTHERN & EASTERN RAIL
TOUR DAY EXCURSION
10th August, 1958
Liverpool St. to Carpenders Rd. Curve,
Tottenham, Bishop's Stortford, Braintree,
Witham, Marks Tey, Halstead, Haverill,
Cambridge, Bedford (St. Johns & Midland
Rd.), Harpenden (Central) Heath Park
Halt, Harpenden (Central) & St. Pancras
For conditions see over

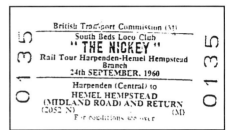

British Transport Commission (M)
South Beds Loco Club
"THE NICKEY"
Rail Tour Harpenden-Hemel Hempstead
Branch
24th SEPTEMBER, 1960
Harpenden (Central) to
HEMEL HEMPSTEAD
(MIDLAND ROAD) AND RETURN
(2052 N)   (M)
For conditions see over

0135   0135

C. 294 R.

Special River Illuminations and Floodlighting

EVENING EXCURSIONS

SATURDAYS, JULY 18th, AUGUST 15th, and SEPTEMBER 12th

TO

BEDFORD

FROM				Times of Departure	THIRD CLASS RETURN FARES	
				p.m.	s.	d.
HEMEL HEMPSTEAD	...	...	...	5 25	1	6
GODWINS HALT	...	...	...	5 32		
BEAUMONTS HALT	...	...	...	5 38		
REDBOURN	...	...	...	5 42	1	3
ROUNDWOOD HALT	...	...	...	5 50		
BEDFORD	...	...	arr.	6 40	—	

Passengers change at Harpenden in each direction.

RETURN ARRANGEMENTS.

Passengers return the same day only by Special Train from BEDFORD at 10.30 p.m.

Children under three years of age, free ; three years and under fourteen, half-fares.

CONDITIONS OF ISSUE OF EXCURSION TICKETS AND OTHER TICKETS
AT LESS THAN ORDINARY FARE.

These Tickets are issued subject to the Notices and Conditions shown in the Company's current
Time Tables.

For LUGGAGE ALLOWANCES also see Time Tables.

PLEASE RETAIN THIS BILL FOR REFERENCE.

Further information may be obtained on application to any LMS Station, Office or to
H. E. ROBERTS, District Passenger Manager, Euston Station, London, N.W.I.

(Telephone : Museum 2900.)

June, 1936.   E.R.O. 53302.   ASHTON DAVIES, Chief Commercial Manager.

Obtain the "Holidays by LMS" Guide, and plan your Holidays now.

LONDON MIDLAND AND SCOTTISH RAILWAY

EARLY CLOSING HALF-DAY TRIPS.

COOK'S
CHEAP TICKETS

WILL BE ISSUED FROM

HEMEL HEMPSTED
Every WEDNESDAY & SATURDAY

Commencing AUGUST 18th, 1923,
UNTIL FURTHER NOTICE as under :—

TO	Times of Departure.	RETURN FARES	
		First Class	Third Class
		s. d.	s. d.
Harpenden ...	By any ordinary train at or after 12.0 noon up to 3.30 p.m. incl.	—	1 0
Luton ...		2 5	1 6
Bedford (Mid.)		6 6	3 11
St. Albans (Mid.)		2 1	1 3
St. Pancras ...		5 8	3 5

RETURN ARRANGEMENTS.
The Tickets will be available for return by any ordinary train
on the day of issue only.

PASSENGERS ARE REQUESTED TO OBTAIN TICKETS IN ADVANCE.
Tickets can be purchased at the STATION.

CONDITIONS OF ISSUE OF TICKETS.
CHILDREN under three years of age, free ; three years and under twelve, half-fares.
NOTICE.—The tickets are not transferable, and will be available on the date of issue only, by
the trains, and at the stations named ; if used on any other date, by any other train, or at any
other station than those named, the tickets will be forfeited and the full ordinary fare charged.
The Company give notice that these tickets are issued at a reduced rate, and subject to the
condition that the Company shall not be liable for any loss, damage, injury, or delay to passengers,
arising from any cause whatsoever.
No luggage allowed.
Should the Company consider it necessary or desirable, from any cause, to alter or cancel these
arrangements, they reserve to themselves the right to do so.

August, 1923.   ARTHUR WATSON, General Manager.

B330-23-F   Thos. Cook & Son, Printers, &c., Ludgate Circus, London, E.C.4.

MP Middleton Press

EVOLVING THE ULTIMATE RAIL ENCYCLOPEDIA

Easebourne Lane, Midhurst, West Sussex.
GU29 9AZ Tel:01730 813169

www.middletonpress.co.uk email:info@middletonpress.co.uk

A-0 906520 B-1 873793 C-1 901706 D-1 904474

OOP Out of print at time of printing - Please check availability BROCHURE AVAILABLE SHOWING NEW TITLES

Index

A
Abergavenny to Merthyr C 91 5
Abertillery and Ebbw Vale Lines D 84 5
Aldgate & Stepney Tramways B 70 7
Allhallows - Branch Line to A 62 2
Alton - Branch Lines to A 11 8
Andover to Southampton A 82 7
Ascot - Branch Lines around A 64 9
Ashburton - Branch Line to B 95 2
Ashford - Steam to Eurostar B 67 7
Ashford to Dover A 48 7
Austrian Narrow Gauge D 04 7
Avonmouth - BL around D 42 X
Aylesbury to Rugby D 91 8
B
Baker Street to Uxbridge D 90 X
Banbury to Birmingham D 27 6
Barking to Southend C 80 X
Barnet & Finchley Tramways B 93 6
Barry - Branch Lines around D 50 0
Basingstoke to Salisbury A 89 4
Bath Green Park to Bristol C 36 2
Bath to Evercreech Junction A 60 6
Bath Tramways B 86 3
Battle over Portsmouth 1940 A 29 0
Battle over Sussex 1940 A 79 7
Bedford to Wellingborough D 31 4
Betwixt Petersfield & Midhurst A 94 0
Blitz over Sussex 1941-42 B 35 9
Bodmin - Branch Lines around B 83 9
Bognor at War 1939-45 B 59 6
Bombers over Sussex 1943-45 B 51 0
Bournemouth & Poole Trys B 47 2
Bournemouth to Evercreech Jn A 46 0
Bournemouth to Weymouth A 57 6
Bournemouth Trolleybuses C 10 9
Bradford Trolleybuses D 19 5
Branch Line to Hemel Hempstead D 88 8
Brecon to Neath D 43 8
Brecon to Newport D 16 0
Brickmaking in Sussex B 19 7
Brightons Tramways B 02 2 OOP
Brighton to Eastbourne A 16 9
Brighton to Worthing A 03 7
Brighton Trolleybuses D 34 9
Bristols Tramways B 57 X
Bristol to Taunton D 03 9
Bromley South to Rochester B 23 5
Bromsgrove to Birmingham D 87 X
Bromsgrove to Gloucester D 73 X
Brunel - A railtour of his achievements D 74 8
Bude - Branch Line to B 29 4
Burnham to Evercreech Jn A 68 1
Burton & Ashby Tramways C 51 6
C
Camberwell & West Norwood Tys B 22 7
Cambridge to Ely D 55 1
Canterbury - Branch Lines around B 58 8
Cardiff Trolleybuses D 64 0
Caterham & Tattenham Corner B 25 1
Changing Midhurst C 15 X
Chard and Yeovil - BLs around C 30 3
Charing Cross to Dartford A 75 4
Charing Cross to Orpington A 96 7
Cheddar - Branch Line to B 90 1
Cheltenham to Andover C 43 5
Cheltenham to Redditch D 81 0
Chesterfield Tramways D 37 3
Chesterfield Trolleybuses D 51 9
Chichester to Portsmouth A 14 2
Clapham & Streatham Trys B 97 9 OOP
Clapham Junction - 50 yrs C 06 0 OOP
Clapham Junction to Beckenham Jn B 36 7
Clevedon & Portishead - BLs to D 18 7
Collectors Trains, Trolleys & Trams D 29 2
Colonel Stephens D62 4
Cornwall Narrow Gauge D 56 X
Crawley to Littlehampton A 34 7
Cromer - Branch Lines around C 26 5
Croydons Tramways B 42 1
Croydons Trolleybuses B 73 1 OOP
Croydon to East Grinstead B 48 0
Crystal Palace (HL) & Catford Loop A 87 8
D
Darlington Trolleybuses D 33 0
Dartford to Sittingbourne B 34 0
Derby Tramways D 17 9
Derby Trolleybuses C 72 9
Derwent Valley - Branch Line to the D 06 3
Didcot to Banbury D 02 0
Didcot to Swindon C 84 2
Didcot to Winchester C 13 3
Dorset & Somerset Narrow Gauge D 76 4
Douglas to Peel C 88 5
Douglas to Port Erin C 55 9
Douglas to Ramsey D 39 X
Dovers Tramways B 24 3
Dover to Ramsgate A 78 9
E
Ealing to Slough C 42 7
Eastbourne to Hastings A 27 4 OOP
East Cornwall Mineral Railways D 22 5
East Croydon to Three Bridges A 53 3
East Grinstead - Branch Lines to A 07 X
East Ham & West Ham Tramways B 52 9
East Kent Light Railway A 61 4 OOP
East London - Branch Lines of C 44 3
East London Line B 80 4
East Ridings Secret Resistance D 21 7
Edgware & Willesden Tramways C 18 4
Effingham Junction - BLs around A 74 6
Eltham & Woolwich Tramways B 74 X OOP
Ely to Kings Lynn C 53 2
Ely to Norwich C 90 7
Embankment & Waterloo Tramways B 41 3
Enfield & Wood Green Trys C 03 6 OOP
Enfield Town & Palace Gates - BL to D 32 2
Epsom to Horsham A 30 4
Euston to Harrow & Wealdstone C 89 3
Exeter & Taunton Tramways B 32 4
Exeter to Barnstaple B 15 4
Exeter to Newton Abbot C 49 4
Exeter to Tavistock B 69 3
Exmouth - Branch Lines to B 00 6
F
Fairford - Branch Line to A 52 5
Falmouth, Helston & St. Ives - BL to C 74 5
Fareham to Salisbury A 67 3
Faversham to Dover B 05 7
Felixstowe & Aldeburgh - BL to D 20 9
Fenchurch Street to Barking C 20 6
Festiniog - 50 yrs of enterprise C 83 4
Festiniog in the Fifties B 68 5
Festiniog in the Sixties B 91 X
Finsbury Park to Alexandra Palace C 02 8
Frome to Bristol B 77 4
Fulwell - Trams, Trolleys & Buses D 11 X
G
Gloucester to Bristol D 35 7
Gloucester to Cardiff D 66 7
Gosport & Horndean Trys B 92 8
Gosport - Branch Lines around A 36 3
Great Yarmouth Tramways D 13 6
Greece Narrow Gauge D 72 1
Greenwich & Dartford Tramways B 14 6 OOP
Grimsby & Cleethorpes Trolleybuses D 86 1
Guildford to Redhill A 63 0 OOP
H
Hammersmith & Hounslow Trys C 33 8
Hampshire Narrow Gauge D 36 5
Hampshire Waterways A 84 3 OOP
Hampstead & Highgate Tramways B 53 7
Harrow to Watford D 14 4
Hastings to Ashford A 37 1
Hastings Tramways B 18 9
Hastings Trolleybuses B 81 2 OOP
Hawkhurst - Branch Line to A 66 5
Hayling - Branch Line to A 12 6
Haywards Heath to Seaford A 28 2
Henley, Windsor & Marlow - BL to C77 X
Hereford to Newport D 54 3
Hexham to CarlisleD 75 6
Hitchin to Peterborough D 07 1
Holborn & Finsbury Tramways B 79 0
Holborn Viaduct to Lewisham A 81 9
Horsham - Branch Lines to A 02 9
Huddersfield Trolleybuses C 92 3
Hull Tramways D60 8
Hull Trolleybuses D 24 1
Huntingdon - Branch Lines around A 93 2
I
Ilford & Barking Tramways B 61 8
Ilford to Shenfield C 97 4
Ilfracombe - Branch Line to B 21 9
Ilkeston & Glossop Tramways D 40 3
Industrial Rlys of the South East A 09 6
Ipswich to Saxmundham C 41 9
Ipswich Trolleybuses D 59 4
Isle of Wight Lines - 50 yrs C 12 5
K
Keighley Tramways & Trolleybuses D 83 7
Kent & East Sussex Waterways A 72 X
Kent Narrow Gauge C 45 1
Kent Seaways - Hoys to Hovercraft D 79 9
Kingsbridge - Branch Line to C 98 2
Kingston & Hounslow Loops A 83 5 OOP
Kingston & Wimbledon Tramways B 56 1
Kingswear - Branch Line to C 17 6
L
Lambourn - Branch Line to C 70 2
Launceston & Princetown - BL to C 19 2
Lewisham & Catford Tramways B 26 X OOP
Lewisham to Dartford A 92 4
Lines around Wimbledon B 75 8
Liverpool Street to Chingford D 01 2
Liverpool Street to Ilford C 34 6
Liverpool Tramways - Eastern C 04 4
Liverpool Tramways - Northern C 46 X
Liverpool Tramways - Southern C 23 0
London Bridge to Addiscombe B 20 0
London Bridge to East Croydon A 58 4
London Chatham & Dover Railway A 88 6
London Termini - Past and Proposed D 00 4
London to Portsmouth Waterways B 43 X
Longmoor - Branch Lines to A 41 X
Looe - Branch Line to C 22 2
Lyme Regis - Branch Line to A 45 2
Lynton - Branch Line to B 04 9
M
Maidstone & Chatham Tramways B 40 5
Maidstone Trolleybuses C 00 1 OOP
March - Branch Lines around B 09 X
Margate & Ramsgate Tramways C 52 4
Marylebone to Rickmansworth D49 7
Midhurst - Branch Lines around A 49 5
Midhurst - Branch Lines to A 01 0 OOP
Military Defence of West Sussex A 23 1
Military Signals, South Coast C 54 0
Minehead - Branch Line to A 80 0
Mitcham Junction Lines B 01 4
Mitchell & company C 59 1
Monmouthshire Eastern Valleys D 71 3
Moreton-in-Marsh to Worcester D 26 8
Moretonhampstead - BL to C 27 3
Mountain Ash to Neath D 80 2
N
Newbury to Westbury C 66 4
Newcastle to Hexham D 69 1
Newcastle Trolleybuses D 78 0
Newport (IOW) - Branch Lines to A 26 6
Newquay - Branch Lines to C 71 0
Newton Abbot to Plymouth C 60 5
Northern France Narrow Gauge C 75 3
North East German Narrow Gauge D 44 6
North Kent Tramways B 44 8
North London Line B 94 4
North Woolwich - BLs around C 65 6
Norwich Tramways C 40 0
Nottinghamshire & Derbyshire T/B D 63 2
Nottinghamshire & Derbyshire T/W D 53 5
O
Orpington to Tonbridge B 03 0 OOP
Oxford to Bletchley D57 8
Oxford to Moreton-in-Marsh D 15 2
P
Paddington to Ealing C 37 0
Paddington to Princes Risborough C 81 8
Padstow - Branch Line to B 54 5
Plymouth - BLs around B 98 7
Plymouth to St. Austell C 63 X
Pontypool to Mountain Ash D 65 9
Porthmadog 1954-94 - BL around B 31 6
Porthmadog to Blaenau B 50 2 OOP
Portmadoc 1923-46 - BL around B 13 8
Portsmouths Tramways B 72 3
Portsmouth to Southampton A 31 2
Portsmouth Trolleybuses C 73 7
Potters Bar to Cambridge D 70 5
Princes Risborough - Branch Lines to D 05 5
Princes Risborough to Banbury C 85 0
R
Railways to Victory C 16 8/7 OOP
Reading to Basingstoke B 27 8
Reading to Didcot C 79 6
Reading to Guildford A 47 9 OOP
Reading Tramways B 87 1
Reading Trolleybuses C 05 2
Redhill to Ashford A 73 8
Return to Blaenau 1970-82 C 64 8
Rickmansworth to Aylesbury D 61 6
Roman Roads of Hampshire D 67 5
Roman Roads of Surrey C 61 3
Roman Roads of Sussex C 48 6
Romneyrail C 32 X
Ryde to Ventnor A 19 3
S
Salisbury to Westbury B 39 1
Salisbury to Yeovil B 06 5 OOP
Saxmundham to Yarmouth C 69 9
Saxony Narrow Gauge D 47 0
Seaton & Eastbourne Tramways B 76 6 OOP
Seaton & Sidmouth - Branch Lines to A 95 9
Secret Sussex Resistance B 82 0
SECR Centenary album C 11 7
Selsey - Branch Line to A 04 5
Sheerness - Branch Lines around B 16 2
Shepherds Bush to Uxbridge T/Ws C 28 1
Shrewsbury - Branch Line to A 86 X
Sierra Leone Narrow Gauge D 28 4
Sittingbourne to Ramsgate A 90 8
Slough to Newbury C 56 7
Solent - Creeks, Crafts & Cargoes D 52 7
Southamptons Tramways B 33 2
Southampton to Bournemouth A 42 8
Southend-on-Sea Tramways B 28 6
Southern France Narrow Gauge C 47 8
Southwark & Deptford Tramways B 38 3
Southwold - Branch Line to A 15 0
South Eastern & Chatham Railways C 08 7
South London Line B 46 4
South London Tramways 1903-33 D 10 1
South London Tramways 1933-52 D 89 6
St. Albans to Bedford D 08 X
St. Austell to Penzance C 67 2
St. Pancras to Barking D 68 3
St. Pancras to St. Albans C 78 8
Stamford Hill Tramways B 85 5
Steaming through Cornwall B 30 8 OOP
Steaming through Kent A 13 4 OOP
Steaming through the Isle of Wight A 56 8
Steaming through West Hants A 69 X
Stratford upon avon to Birmingham D 772
Stratford upon Avon to Cheltenham C 25 7
Strood to Paddock Wood B 12 X OOP
Surrey Home Guard C 57 5
Surrey Narrow Gauge C 87 7
Surrey Waterways A 51 7 OOP
Sussex Home Guard C 24 9
Sussex Narrow Gauge C 68 0
Sussex Shipping Sail, Steam & Motor D 23 3
Swanley to Ashford B 45 6
Swindon to Bristol C 96 6
Swindon to Gloucester D46 2
Swindon to Newport D 30 6
Swiss Narrow Gauge C 94 X
T
Talyllyn - 50 years C 39 7
Taunton to Barnstaple B 60 X
Taunton to Exeter C 82 6
Tavistock to Plymouth B 88 X
Tees-side Trolleybuses D 58 6
Tenterden - Branch Line to A 21 5
Thanet's Tramways B 11 1 OOP
Three Bridges to Brighton A 35 5
Tilbury Loop C 86 9
Tiverton - Branch Lines around C 62 1
Tivetshall to Beccles D 41 1
Tonbridge to Hastings A 44 4
Torrington - Branch Lines to B 37 5
Tunbridge Wells - Branch Lines to A 32 0
Twickenham & Kingston Trys C 35 4
Two-Foot Gauge Survivors C 21 4 OOP
U
Upwell - Branch Line to B 64 2
V
Victoria & Lambeth Tramways B 49 9
Victoria to Bromley South A 98 3
Victoria to East Croydon A 40 1 OOP
Vivarais C 31 1 OOP
W
Walthamstow & Leyton Tramways B 65 0
Waltham Cross & Edmonton Trys C 07 9
Wandsworth & Battersea Tramways B 63 4
Wantage - Branch Line to D 25 X
Wareham to Swanage - 50 yrs D 09 8
War on the Line A 10 X
War on the Line VIDEO + 88 0
Waterloo to Windsor A 54 1
Waterloo to Woking A 38 X
Watford to Leighton Buzzard D 45 4
Wenford Bridge to Fowey C 09 5
Westbury to Bath B 55 3
Westbury to Taunton C 76 1
West Cornwall Mineral Railways D 48 9
West Croydon to Epsom B 08 1
West London - Branch Lines of C 50 8
West London Line B 84 7
West Sussex Waterways A 24 X OOP
West Wiltshire - Branch Lines of D 12 8
Weymouth - Branch Lines around A 65 7
Willesden Junction to Richmond B 71 5
Wimbledon to Beckenham C 58 3
Wimbledon to Epsom B 62 6
Wimborne - Branch Lines around A 97 5
Wisbech - Branch Lines around C 01 X
Wisbech 1800-1901 C 93 1
Woking to Alton A 59 2
Woking to Portsmouth A 25 8
Woking to Southampton A 55 X
Wolverhampton Trolleybuses D 85 3
Woolwich & Dartford Trolleys B 66 9
Worcester to Hereford D 38 1
Worthing to Chichester A 06 1
Y
Yeovil - 50 yrs change C 38 9
Yeovil to Dorchester A 76 2 OOP
Yeovil to Exeter A 91 6
York Tramways & Trolleybuses D 82 9